Seeds
and Plants

Adria F. Klein

DOMINIE PRESS
Pearson Learning Group

ISBN 0-7685-0564-X

Printed in Singapore

17 V0ZF 14 13 12

Dominie
Press

Pearson Learning Group

1-800-321-3106
www.pearsonlearning.com

Table of Contents

Dad and I bought some seeds.
We planted the seeds
in little pots.
We kept the pots inside
to keep them warm.
We put them in the sun
by a window.

6

The seeds started to grow.
They grew into little plants.
When the ground in the garden
was warm, we dug lots of holes.
We put plant food in the holes.
We planted our tomato plants
in the holes.

Everyday, I watered
the tomatoes.
I watched them grow.
In one month, the tomato plants
were much bigger.

In two months, the tomato plants had flowers.

Soon, the flowers became
little tomatoes.
The little tomatoes grew
and grew.

I picked my first tomato.
It tasted so sweet.
All summer, I got
to pick tomatoes.
I picked lots of tomatoes.

Soon, fall came.
There were no more flowers
growing on the tomato plants.
There were no more tomatoes.

Winter came.
Dad and I dug up
the tomato plants.
But the ground will be
warm again in the spring.
Dad and I will plant
more tomatoes.

Picture Glossary

flowers:

tomato plants:

pots:

tomatoes:

Index